THE LOS ANGELES RAMS

Published by Creative Education, Inc., 123 South Broad Street, Mankato, Minnesota 56001

Copyright © 1986 by Creative Education, Inc. International copyrights reserved in all countries. No part of this book may be reproduced in any form without written permission from the publisher. Printed in the United States.

Library of Congress Catalog Card No.: 85-72618

ISBN: 0-88682-036-7

THE LOS ANGELES RAMS

JAMES R. ROTHAUS

CREATIVE EDUCATION

THE SHOW BIZ RAMS

They are a bright and brassy team, full of surprises. Their home is Southern California, land of movie stars, surfers, sunshine and smog. In bustling Los Angeles, where life bangs forward in the fast lane, the Rams' "flash and bash" playing style fits right in.

Few players in the NFL have ever run faster—or farther— than the Rams' super-nova running back, Eric Dickerson.

Defense? A string of menacing Ram linebackers, including recent standouts like "Jammin' Jim" Collins, have tackled more bad guys than all the Hollywood stuntmen combined.

Finally, if you like a good cliff-hanger, check out Coach John Robinson's record. When it comes to directing an exciting surprise ending, Robinson deserves the Oscar.

Over the past four decades, the Rams have played to record crowds, won 13 division crowns and captured the National Conference title on two occasions. With a record like that, can the world championship be far away? Decide for yourself. Come with us, now, as we reach back into the stacks for some of the most exciting reruns in NFL history!

Did you know?

Nolan Cromwell has been the Rams' holder on all place-kicks since his rookie season (1977). He is notorious for his electrifying fake field-goal dashes.

The great Bob Waterfield was a star at UCLA and a rookie sensation with the old Cleveland Rams. He was one of the first passers to use the long bomb. Waterfield was a mainstay of the LA Rams, an outstanding punter, runner and field leader. He is a member of Football's Hall of Fame.

> **Did you know?**
>
> *Wide receiver Preston Dennard averages about 40 catches per season. In the off-seasons, Dennard has worked with his mother to produce gospel concerts and has recorded a progressive rhythm and blues album as a solo vocalist.*

THE CHAMPS HEAD WEST

Back in 1945, there was no Super Bowl. In fact there were no Los Angeles Rams. Back then, the Rams played in Cleveland, Ohio and were owned by multimillionaire Dan Reeves.

Nothing irritated Reeves more than losing, and that's exactly what the Rams were known for in the early days.

From 1937 to 1944, the Cleveland Rams rarely rose above the .500 level. Fans around Ohio showed little interest in pro football, opting instead to watch the college game at nearby Ohio State.

By 1945, Reeves was ready to move his team to new surroundings. Little did he know that rookie quarterback Bob Waterfield would boost the Rams to new heights that season.

Waterfield's pinpoint passing led Cleveland to the NFL championship in 1945, and the fans began flocking to gigantic Municipal Stadium. But Reeves had already made his decision; the Rams were going west...to Los Angeles.

Somehow, the Rams lost their championship touch during the move. The team was just 6-4-1 in its first season in the sun. Reeves hired and fired three coaches in an effort to get a winning club. As general manager, he instituted a new scouting system to help recruit players. By 1949, both moves combined to produce a winner.

Coach Clark Shaughnessy directed the Rams to an 8-2-2 mark that season, good enough for first place in

Elroy Hirsch was best-known for catching the ball at a dead run. His agility on the field was unmatched until Gale Sayers came along. Hirsch was a star for the Rams for 9 years, retiring in 1957. He is a member of the Hall of Fame.

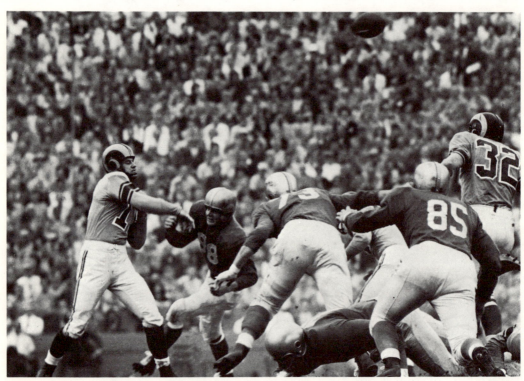

Quarterback Norm Van Brocklin lofts a pass out of reach of a pack of Detroit Lions. Called the Dutchman, he starred for the Rams and later for the Philadelphia Eagles. Then he coached the Minnesota Vikings and the Atlanta Falcons. He is a Hall-of-Famer.

the Western Division. Part of Shaughnessy's secret formula was a 1-2 QB punch. He might start the game with Waterfield. Then, without warning, he would insert rookie passing whiz Norm Van Brocklin.

Van Brocklin's favorite target was Elroy "Crazylegs" Hirsch. Elroy was a peerless receiver with a weird style of running. Nobody could catch forward passes like Crazylegs!

Reeves' bright ideas weren't limited to scouting. In a move to capitalize on the popularity of his team, the Rams' owner arranged to have road games televised. It was a first for pro football. Fans filled the Coliseum for home games, then crowded around their TV sets to watch the Rams play on the road. Soon the Rams were the biggest box office hit in the NFL.

Of course, Los Angeles fans liked what they saw. The Rams were once again in first place, thanks to the record-setting ways of Waterfield and end Tom Fears.

Now, they would travel to Cleveland to face the Browns in the league title game.

Many of the Cleveland fans remembered when the Rams had been the "home" team. So now the stands were divided between supporters of the Browns and their familiar visitors. Late in the game, after Waterfield passed to Fears for the go-ahead TD, it appeared the Rams were again going back to California with the championship trophy. But the Browns stormed back. There were only 30 seconds remaining when Cleveland kicker Lou Groza trotted onto the field with the Rams leading, 28-27.

Groza eyed his target, and then kicked away. The ball sailed cleanly through the uprights. Cleveland had won,

Did you know?

Quarterback Jeff Kemp, who has come a long way since being signed as a free agent in 1981, is the son of former NFL quarterback Jack Kemp, now a U.S. Congressman.

Did you know?

Eleven former Rams have already been enshrined in the Pro Football Hall-of-Fame: Dutch Clark, Tom Fears, Sid Gillman, Elroy "Crazylegs" Hirsch, Deacon Jones, Ollie Matson, Merlin Olsen, Dan Reeves, Andy Robustelli, Norm Van Brocklin and Bob Waterfield!

30-28. That was one of the greatest championship games ever, but an even better contest was played the following year. Here's what happened:

In 1951, the Rams were again Western Division champions, this time under the direction of new head coach Joe Stydahar. That year, Los Angeles boasted a fine passing attack led by Waterfield, Van Brocklin and Crazylegs. But it had also added a new "Bull Elephant Backfield." Burly players such as Tank Younger, Dick Hoerner and Vitamin T. Smith ran over would-be tacklers, rather than around them.

Once again, the opponent in the championship game was Cleveland, but this time the game was to be played in the Southern California sunshine.

With a dry ball to grip, Waterfield opened up the passing lanes to Fears and Hirsch. To finish the drive, Waterfield handed to Hoerner who bulled in for the touchdown.

Moments later Cleveland's Groza stunned the Rams and the crowd by booting a record 52-yard field goal. With Los Angeles still in shock, Browns QB Otto Graham flipped to Dub Jones for a TD and a 10-7 lead.

In the third quarter, the Rams scooped up a Cleveland fumble and turned it into a touchdown. Los Angeles led, 14-10. Van Brocklin and Waterfield then teamed up to increase the lead. Van Brocklin moved the club downfield before Waterfield, who doubled as the team's kicker, banged in a field goal to make it 17-10.

Time was running out on Cleveland in the fourth quarter when Graham tied the score, 17-17. With only seven minutes left, Van Brocklin went for broke. It was third down and three yards to go on the L.A. 27. The

Tom Fears makes the catch. The talented end played for the Rams from 1948 until 1956. He was inducted into the Hall of Fame in 1970.

"Dutchman" faded back to pass, then heaved a rainbow. The ball sailed into the hazy blue sky. It traveled 40, 50, 60 yards! Finally it came down...right into the waiting arms of Fears. It was a Rams touchdown, and Los Angeles had its first championship, 24-17!

ROUGH ROAD AHEAD

Coach Stydahar was one of those natural-born leaders. He was gruff and tough, but warmhearted, much like Vince Lombardi. Like Lombardi, Stydahar was also a great judge of men. He knew how each player could be persuaded to give his best.

Stydahar's top assistant, Hamp Pool, supplied much of the razzle-dazzle to the Rams' offense. Pool's trickery was praised by local newspapers. But when Pool took that trickery to the head coaching position in 1952, it backfired. Pool's complex, scientific game plans—comparable to Tom Landry's coaching at Dallas today—were difficult for the players to learn and accept. Some players actually asked to be traded. It was remarkable that the Rams still managed to make the playoffs.

In one trade alone, Pool peddled 11 players to Dallas for a rookie named Les Richter, who never panned out. To make matters worse, Waterfield retired and All-Pro defensive back Dick "Night Train" Lane left to join the Cardinals.

The last remaining star from the many who had played on the 1951 championship team was Norm Van Brocklin. His cluth passing enabled Los Angeles to finish a respect-

Did you know?

Yikes! In 1960, the great Elroy Hirsch replaced Pete Rozelle as Rams general manager—and "Crazylegs" was loose in the Rams front office! Elroy did a magnificent job until 1969 when he finally left the Rams after 20 years of service as a player and executive.

Dick "Night Train" Lane set an NFL record in 1952, intercepting 14 passes and bringing them back 298 yards. He scored two touchdowns. Night Train later played for the Chicago Cardinals and the Detroit Lions.

> **Did you know?**
>
> *Old-timers will never forget beloved Bill Granholm who signed on as the Rams' equipment manager in 1950 and continued faithfully in that position for the next 18 seasons!*

able 8-3-1 in '53. But in 1954, when the Rams slipped to 6-5-1, Reeves exploded in anger, firing Pool and his entire staff. After a long search, Reeves hired Coach Sid Gillman to lead the team.

Gillman came from the University of Cincinnati, a small college whose football program had blossomed under his direction. The Rams hoped that Gillman, their fifth coach in 11 years, would grow the same kind of program in Los Angeles. Sure enough, the Gillman-led Rams took the conference championship for the first time in four years.

Give credit to Van Brocklin who didn't have an off-day all season. But things were different on the day of the championship game. It seemed that the Cleveland Browns had brought their rainy skies with them from Ohio. Instead of sunglasses and tanning lotion, the Coliseum crowd brought umbrellas.

Rain meant trouble for the pass-happy Rams. The Browns, on the other hand, were right at home in this kind of weather. Otto Graham, the Cleveland QB who had gone into a brief "retirement" earlier in the season, was back at the helm for his final game. Nothing, it seemed, would stand between him and another championship.

Throughout the game, Graham sprayed a torrent of perfect passes. He scored on a 15-yard run and a quarterback sneak. When Cleveland coach Paul Brown took Graham out late in the last quarter, the score was Cleveland 38, Los Angeles 14. It was Graham's last game, and the great California fans gave him a standing ovation.

For the Rams, however, there was nothing but gloom. Their defeat in the championship game was a sign of

Ken Konz (left) of the Browns leaps to intercept a pass intended for the Rams' Skeet Quihlan during the 1955 NFL championship game.

Tank Younger (35) was a stalwart of the Rams' Bull Elephant Backfield.

Among the stars who played for the Rams was Ollie Matson (33), one of the first of the big, strong running backs. Matson was unable to help the sagging Rams when he arrived in Los Angeles in 1959, the result of a 9-player trade with Chicago. Matson is a member of Football's Hall of Fame.

things to come.

The big skid started in 1956. Norm Van Brocklin played inconsistently. Coach Gillman put in rookie quarterback Bill Wade, but Wade was too raw. The Rams finished the season in the cellar.

They did better in 1957, finishing 6-6-0. But Van Brocklin was still in the doldrums and he retired. Later, he was traded to Philadelphia where he bounced back to lead the lowly Eagles to a championship.

But there would be no championship for the Rams in the years that followed. After an 8-4-0 season in 1958, they plummeted to 2-10-0 in 1959. Gillman resigned. Bob Waterfield took over for two seasons. Then Harland Svare led the Rams from 1962 until 1965. Neither Waterfield nor Svare could muster a winning record.

THE FUTURE IS NOW

Dan Reeves, who had sold part of his stock earlier, regained full ownership of the Rams in 1962. With attendance down, Reeves made a brilliant move in 1965 by luring George Allen from the Chicago Bears to be the new head coach of the Rams.

Most new coaches plan on several years of rebuilding to produce a winning team. Not George Allen. Slow wasn't his style. He didn't care about promising young draft choices. He wanted experienced men who could play for him right away.

"I want to win today," explained Allen, a former assistant with Chicago's 1963 championship team. "I don't

Did you know?

In 1983, Eric Dickerson ran with the ball 390 times. That's nearly 100 more carries than the previous season-high set by Lawrence McCutcheon in 1977!

> **Did you know?**
>
> *Quarterback Bob Waterfield threw five touchdown passes in a single 1949 match-up with the old New York Bulldogs. A year earlier Waterfield had played a game against the Packers in which he was intercepted seven times. Ah, the ups and downs of football!*

like waiting. It's not my style to plan for the future. To me, the future is now!"

Allen traded and juggled players, demanding 110 percent from those who stayed. And the team responded by finishing 1966 with a record of 8-6-0—their best showing since 1958.

In 1967, the Rams butted their way past Vince Lombardi's mighty Green Bay Packers in the crucial 13th game of the season. Just 54 seconds remained when the Rams blocked a Packer punt, recovered the ball and scored a touchdown.

The Rams defeated Baltimore in the last game to win the division with a fine 10-3-1 mark. But the Super Bowl would remain just a dream as Green Bay avenged their earlier loss by beating the Rams in the playoffs.

Allen's bread-and-butter was his defense. He had made the Chicago Bears into the famed Monsters of Midway. Now, in Los Angeles, he had built the "Fearsome Foursome" of Rosey Grier, Merlin Olsen, Deacon Jones and Lamar Lundy.

"Until we came along," said Olsen, a living legend at defensive tackle for 14 years, "most fans only looked to offensive players for excitement. The emergence of our line brought some attention over to the defense. We influenced the entire sport. It was fun knowing every time we went on the field we were the guys who were going to make something happen."

On offense, the guy who made things happen was quarterback Roman Gabriel, the league's Most Valuable Player in 1969 when he tossed 24 touchdowns as the Rams went 11-3. In their first playoff game, Gabriel and the Rams faced the physical Minnesota Vikings in bitter-

Talented quarterback Roman Gabriel (18) joined the Rams in 1961 and was coached by Harland Svare. He was well-seasoned when George Allen took over the team in 1966 and turned it into a winner. Gabriel was MVP of the league in 1969.

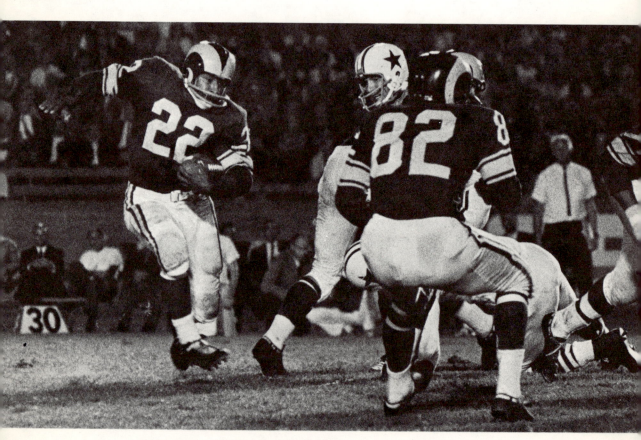

Hippity hoppity — and Dick Bass (22) goes for yardage against Dallas. He was the top rusher in 1966.

cold Bloomington, Minnesota.

Trailing 21-20 late in the fourth quarter, Gabriel got the Rams going. They had driven to the Viking 25 when the L.A. quarterback called a pass on third down—at least he thought it was third down. An official had forgotten to change the down marker, so it was really fourth down. Gabriel threw incomplete, and—to his dismay—the Rams handed the ball over to Minnesota. The Vikings later added a safety to win, 23-20.

Allen, who had experienced some run-ins with Chicago owner George Halas, began warring with Reeves following the 1969 season. When the Rams failed to make the playoffs in 1970 (despite a credible 9-4-1 record), Reeves gave Allen the axe.

L.A. YOUTH MOVEMENT

In 1971, George Allen departed for the nation's capital to coach the Redskins. In his place, Reeves hired the popular UCLA coach, Tommy Prothro. It was the last move Reeves ever made for the Rams. He died unexpectedly a few days later.

Prothro was the exact opposite of Allen. He had no use for "over-the-hill" veterans. As a result, he traded many players to Allen at Washington. Younger players began appearing in key roles for the Rams. Isiah Robertson, a tough young linebacker, and Willie Ellison were two of those players.

Under Allen, the "old" Rams had seldom run the ball. Prothro, however, chose to use a more balanced

Did you know?

The Rams believe in searching for gold nuggets in their own backyard. Heading into the 1985 season, there were 14 Rams who had played their collegiate ball at California colleges!

> **Did you know?**
>
> *Eric Dickerson loves to explode for the long one. Among his 17 touchdowns as a senior at SMU were runs of 80, 80, 79, 70, 63 and 62 yards!*

attack, meaning more carries for Ellison, the young halfback. Ellison became the first Los Angeles runner to reach the celebrated 1,000-yard plateau in 1971, with nearly one-fourth of those yards coming in a single game against New Orleans. On the first play of the game, Ellison showed his brilliant breakaway speed by bolting 80 yards for a touchdown. And he just kept running, until he gained a league record 247 yards in the 45-28 victory!

July 14, 1972. That day, in the most bizarre transaction in NFL history, new Los Angeles owner Robert Irsay swapped the entire Rams organization for Caroll Rosenbloom's Baltimore Colts! All the players stayed in place, only the owners moved in this deal.

Rosenbloom was a shrewd but genial millionaire who had built Baltimore into Super Bowl champions in 1971. He had also been a close friend of Dan Reeves and, like Reeves, Rosenbloom liked to take a hand in running his team. The new owner's first big move was to fire Prothro after a lackluster 6-7-1 season in 1972. More moves followed.

Rosenbloom acted swiftly, overhauling the Rams in a matter of weeks. He hand-picked Detroit assistant Chuck Knox to be the new head coach. Roman Gabriel was traded to make room for John Hadl, the passing whiz from the San Diego Chargers. Younger players—men like Jack Youngblood, Jack Reynolds, Lawrence McCutcheon, Larry Brooks and Cullen Bryant—were moved into starting roles.

Ordinarily it takes a few years for a young team to come together, but Hadl's leadership provided the glue. As a result, the Rams compiled a 12-2 record. The team

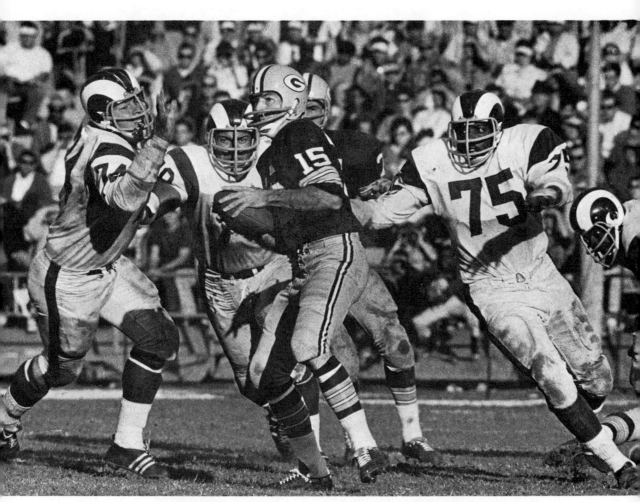

Bart Starr (15) of Green Bay tries to get rid of the ball before the "Fearsome Foursome" defense mashes him flat. Closing in are (l-r) Merlin Olsen, Roger Brown and Deacon Jones. The fourth defender, Lamar Lundy, is almost out of the picture at right.

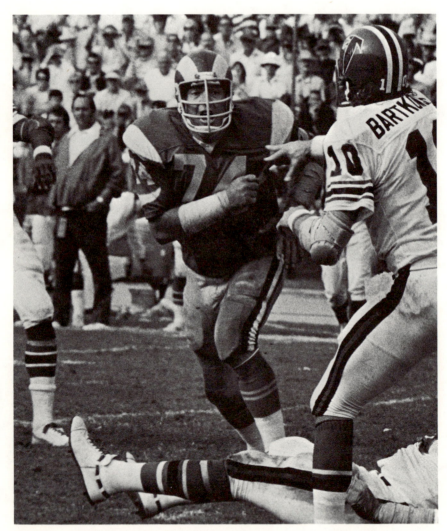

For 14 years, defensive tackle Merlin Olsen anchored the Ram defense. He was co-captain of the team and a perennial All-Star.

won the Western Division, Knox was crowned Coach of the Year. and Hadl was named Player of the Year.

PLAYOFF PRESSURE COOKER

If there was one rap on the Rams, it was that they couldn't win the big ones. They had lost every playoff game from 1952-72, a span of 20 years! Despite the fine running of McCutcheon, Los Angeles fell yet again in 1973, this time to Dallas. Hadl was intercepted three times as the Cowboys rolled to a 17-0 lead before holding on for a 26-17 victory.

Hadl's woes continued into 1974. When the Rams slipped to 3-2 after five games, Coach Knox removed Hadl in favor of a young black quarterback named James Harris.

Before Harris, no black had ever been given an opportunity to be a starting pro quarterback. Harris made the most of his chance. In his first start, he threw two touchdown passes to lead Los Angeles past arch-rival San Francisco, 37-14. Rosenbloom was so impressed with Harris that he traded Hadl to Green Bay the following day.

Harris rewarded Knox and Rosenbloom by directing the Rams to another first-place finish. "I have good feelings about this team," said Rosenbloom. "They show a lot of character. They work harder and they're not as fancy. They earn every win."

The hard work paid off with a first-round playoff victory over Washington, 19-10. But in the NFC title

Did you know?

On September 30, 1984, the Rams defeated the Giants in one of the most peculiar displays of defensive football in recent memory. L.A. held N.Y. to only eight yards rushing for the entire game. Plus, the Rams sacked quarterback Phil Simms five times. Plus, the Rams recorded three safeties on two blocked punts and an end-zone sack!

> **Did you know?**
>
> *Herb Rich intercepted a Dallas, Texans pass in 1952 and returned it for 97 yards. It was a record that would stand until 1980 when Johnnie Johnson snatched a Green Bay pass and returned it for 99 yards!*

game, Minnesota prevailed, 14-10.

Harris had the Rams moving again in 1975 until he suffered a shoulder injury late in the season. Anchored by a defense which allowed opponents less than 10 points per game, young Ron Jaworski took over and guided the Rams into the playoffs with their third straight Western Division championship.

McCutcheon, the muscular running back who was a regular member of the NFL 1,000-yard club, ran wild in the first playoff game, gaining an NFC record 202 yards on 37 trips against St. Louis. The Rams won easily, beating the Cardinals, 34-23. The next week, though, Los Angeles lost another "big one," this time to Dallas, 37-7.

With Harris still injured, Coach Knox turned to a diminutive rookie named Pat Haden to guide the club's fortunes in 1976. Haden, who had quarterbacked the USC Trojans to Rose Bowl wins, made a super effort in taking the Rams to two more divisional titles in 1976-77, but he could not get them into the Super Bowl.

For Chuck Knox, losing in the playoffs was very frustrating. In his five years with the club, the Rams' 54-15-1 regular-record was the best in pro football. In the playoffs, however, they were only 3-5. Knox resigned following the '77 season to coach the Buffalo Bills.

THE YEAR OF THE RAM?

When Knox left, many fans urged Rosenbloom to bring back George Allen. Rosenbloom agreed, but soon

James Harris was the first black quarterback to become a regular starter in the NFL.

realized that he had made a mistake. Once again, Allen immediately began ridding the Rams of young players—the same young guys who had been winning all those ball games for Los Angeles. With team morale sagging, Rosenbloom acted quickly, firing Allen after two pre-season games!

Assistant coach Ray Malavasi, a favorite of the players, was chosen to replace Allen for the remainder of the '78 season. Haden, who liked Malavasi, responded by quarterbacking the team to its sixth division title in six years. This time Minnesota didn't play the stopper. The Rams defeated the Vikings in round one, 34-10. Then, moving to Dallas for the finals, the Rams' balloon burst. Dallas tromped the Rams, 28-0. It was not a game to remember.

The Chinese declared 1979 to be "The Year of the Ram," but no one remembered to tell L.A. Bad fortune shadowed the team from day one. First, the franchise was moved 30 miles south from the Coliseum to Anaheim. Playing in a new stadium, the Rams wouldn't even hold a true home-field advantage that year. Shortly after the move, tragedy struck. Caroll Rosenbloom died in a drowning accident.

The Rams lost five of their first nine games. Then, while leading the club to a satisfying 24-0 win over Seattle, Pat Haden broke his hand on a teammate's helmet. It seemed nothing could go right. Malavasi acquired journeyman Bob Lee from Minnesota to fill the QB slot, but Lee was injured in his second outing.

Now, the the Rams were down to one able-bodied quarterback—seldom-used Vince Ferragamo who had sat on the bench for two seasons. "Vince, I've got all the

Did you know?

One of the most remarkable feats in recent football lore involves iron-man Jack Youngblood. Jack fractured his leg in the first round of the 1979 playoffs, but continued to play. He was fitted with a plastic brace and played every defensive down in the NFC Championship Game and the Super Bowl—with a broken leg!

Gotcha! Three Ram defenders haul down Minnesota's Dave Osborn during the 1974 NFC championship game. The Rams are Jack Reynolds, Larry Brooks and Fred Dryer.

> **Did you know?**
>
> *In 1943, the NFL sent many of its best warriors off to fight World War II. The Rams' ranks were especially hard-hit, so the NFL granted the franchise permission to suspend operations for that particular season!*

confidence in the world that you'll pull us through," said Malavasi. The Los Angeles coach prayed that Ferragamo would stay healthy. If Vince went down, the only other Ram who could handle a snap was Nolan Cromwell, a defensive end who had played a few games at quarterback in college.

Hah! Ferragamo took his share of lumps in the remaining six regular-season games. But—believe it or not—he actually managed to steer the Rams to a seventh consecutive division title.

As usual, the Rams folded in the playoffs, right? Not this time!

They faced the mighty Dallas Cowboys, and the team from Texas quickly went ahead, 16-7. But Ferragamo refused to quit. He rifled a 43-yard TD strike to Jessie and a 50-yard scoring bomb to Billy Waddy to lift the Rams to a 21-19 upset victory.

"No one gave us a chance," smiled an elated Ferragamo after the game, "but our own confidence kept us in there. I think we showed everyone that this is a different Rams team."

The next week, the new "Fearsome Foursome II" held Tampa Bay scoreless and kicker Frank Corral booted three field goals as Los Angeles won the NFC Championship game over Tampa, 9-0. Finally, the Rams were heading to the world championships!

SUPER BOWL XIV

Super Bowl XIV would be played in Pasadena's Rose Bowl, and the Rams were considered heavy underdogs

Ron Jaworski gets away from Card Greg Hartel to score the first Ram TD during the 1975 playoff game.

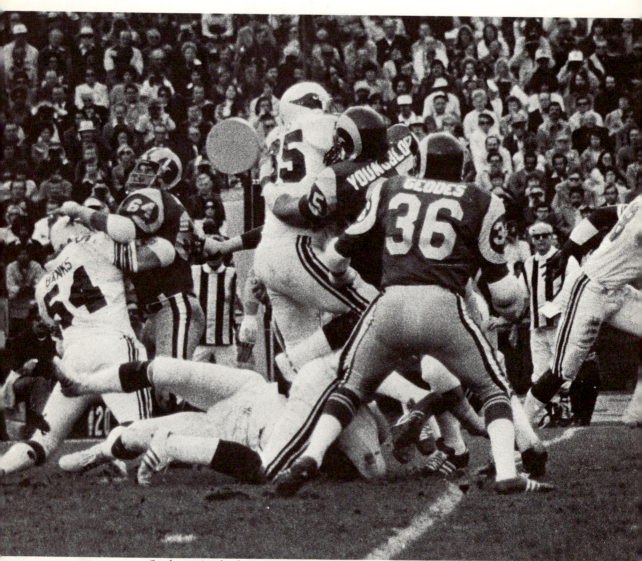
Card running back Jim Otis (35) gets crunched by Los Angeles' Jack Youngblood (85), who reaped many defensive Player-of-the-Year awards in 1975. Other Rams in on the action include Ken Geddes and Jack Reynolds.

to the two-time world champion Pittsburgh Steelers.

Pittsburgh QB, Terry Bradshaw, the league's most experienced playoff quarterback, would be pitted against Vince Ferragamo, one of the least. Fortunately, the Rams had the home-field advantage.

Indeed, more than 103,000 fans packed the Rose Bowl for this battle of David vs. Goliath. They watched as the gutsy Rams grabbed with the teeth and held on in a game that Steeler quarterback Bradshaw would later call, "one of the five toughest games I ever played in."

The first half was a dogfight. Thanks to Corral's gorgeous 45-yard field goal in the final seconds of the second quarter, the Rams went into the locker room with a 16-13 lead at intermission.

Coach Malavasi knew the Rams could not sit on such a slim lead, so he designed a tricky flea-flicker play for the third quarter. Ferragamo handed to McCutcheon on a sweep. Before McCutcheon got to the line, however, he set up and threw 24 yards to Ron Smith for a touchdown. Now, the Rams led 19-17 with only 15 minutes to go.

Bradshaw, the master under pressure, came out firing in the fourth quarter. He hit John Stallworth on a 73-yard pass to put Pittsburgh into the lead, 24-19. Then Pittsburgh's awesome "Steel Curtain" defense descended with a crash. The Rams were stopped, and Steeler fullback Franco Harris punched across another score, sealing a 31-19 win for Pittsburgh.

"I got to tell you," said Bradshaw, as he wiped the sweat from his face after the game, "there was no loser today. Both teams deserve the title. The Rams are one tough club."   Malavasi was proud of his troops. They

Did you know?

Oh, that Rams' defense! In 1974, the L.A. stop-squad allowed the second fewest points in NFL history over a 14-game season (135) and—sure enough—the Rams won their third straight NFC Western title!

> **Did you know?**
>
> *1981 was a great season for Wendell Tyler and his fans, but a bitter-sweet one for Elroy Hirsch's fans. That was the year Tyler tied Hirsch's long-standing record of 17 touchdowns in a single season!*

had confounded all the experts by getting to the Super Bowl, and then almost winning it. "Not even a Hollywood astrologer could have predicted this," joked Malavasi.

When Haden returned in 1980, nearly everyone expected him to reclaim his No. 1 spot. But Ferragamo's confidence was brimming. He believed he was the best QB, and he went out and proved it. In one of the greatest displays in Rams quarterbacking history, Ferragamo threw for 30 touchdown passes that year. On the ground, the explosive Wendell Tyler rushed for 17 touchdowns of his own.

On defense, Jack Youngblood, who had played with a broken leg in Super Bowl XIV, led the L.A. stop-squad. Nolan Cromwell was all over the place, making interceptions, batting down passes and flying through the air for spectacular tackles. It was another great season for the Rams, who finished 11-5. But the Atlanta Falcons, owning a fine 12-4 mark, finally ended L.A.'s seven-year string of Western Division championships.

After the 1980 season, Coach Ray Malavasi talked openly of his frustration. Despite all their hard work and talent, it seemed the Rams were destined to remain second-best. How many times had they fought their way to the top of the ladder, only to be tipped away from the NFL crown at the last minute?

"They say it's bad luck to talk about the Super Bowl," said Malavasi, "but we're doing it anyway. We talk about the Super Bowl at practice, and at our team meetings. We don't talk about 'getting' to the Super Bowl, we talk about 'winning' it. And we don't buy that baloney about bad luck—we think a team makes its own luck."

McCutcheon and Jaworski congratulate each other after the Rams' victory over the Cardinals in the 1975 playoffs.

Coach Chuck Knox (right) along with line coach Ray Prochaska and wide receiver Otto Stowe.

Malavasi put every position up for grabs in 1981. Even the quarterback slot was open. After a salary dispute with Rams owner Georgia Frontiere (Caroll Rosenbloom's widow), Ferragamo had packed his bags and departed for the Canadian Football League. Vying for the position were Jeff Rutledge, Jeff Kemp, Dan Pastorini and Pat Haden, who had recovered from an injury. Unfortunately, none of the four could muster much offense that season, as the Rams swooned to 6-10, missing the playoffs for the first time since 1962.

The road became exceptionally rough for the Rams in 1982. Bert Jones, the all-Pro QB who had come in a trade from Baltimore, injured his neck midway through the season and eventually retired. Ferragamo returned from Canada to take over for Jones, and even passed for 509 yards (the second-highest total in NFL history) in a game against Chicago. In the end, however, the Rams managed only two wins in the strike-shortened season.

JOHN ROBINSON TO THE RESCUE

It was obvious to Georgia Frontiere that the Rams needed a new leader. She had only one person in mind. His name was John Robinson, the man who had led the nearby USC Trojans to three Pacific-10 Conference titles and one collegiate national championship.

"I'm a big fan of Coach Robinson, as is everyone from this part of the country," said Mrs. Frontiere. "I am confident that he will lead the Rams back to the top."

Coach Robinson wasn't shy about making changes.

Did you know?

The Rams entered the 1984 training camp with eleven former No. 1 draft choices on their roster, including Jack Youngblood, Dennis Harrah, George Andrews, Kent Hill, Johnnie Johnson, Mel Owens, Barry Redden, Eric Dickerson, Mike Williams, Gary Jeter and Gary Green!

> **Did you know?**
>
> *Wide receiver Drew Hill will never forget the first regular-season game in Anaheim Stadium. The year was 1980. Drew received the opening kick-off and returned it 98 yards for a Rams touchdown!*

He immediately gave the Rams' offense a totally new look by going to a single running back formation.

"We need a special kind of guy back there," explained Robinson. Indeed. The guy he had in mind was the one-and-only Eric Dickerson, the All-America halfback from Southern Methodist University.

Dickerson was the second player taken in the 1983 draft. He didn't have to compete for the running back position; with the trade of Wendell Tyler, he had it all to himself.

Defensively, Robinson asked Youngblood and Cromwell—Mr. Heart and Mr. Soul—to take new positions in the Rams lineup. "If it will help us win, I'll do it," barked Youngblood.

Ferragamo was once again the quarterback, but now the emphasis was on rushing. Oh, Ferragamo still threw his share of TD passes (22, in fact), but most of the glory went to Dickerson. The bespectacled rookie pounded his way to the NFL rushing title by gaining 1,808 yards and scoring a club record 18 touchdowns!

"Eric Dickerson is the second coming of all the great NFL runners who have ever played this game," wrote Gerome Michaels for INSPORTS Magazine. "I look out there and I see Dickerson, but if I squint my eyes a little, I can see Hugh McElhenny, Ollie Matson, Gale Sayers, Jim Brown and O.J. Simpson, all packed into Dickerson's uniform. He combines all their best moves in a style that is peculiarly his own."

When it came time to wrap up a playoff spot, however, it was the Rams' defense—especially Cromwell and Youngblood—who stole the show from their rookie running back and took matters into their own hands.

Interception! Rams linebacker George Andrews (52) returns one against the frustrated Chargers in a 1984 match-up.

Rams center Doug Smith anchors one of the stingiest offensive lines in the entire NFL against the sack.

Playing against New Orleans in a loser-out situation, Youngblood set the stage early by doing a kamikaze routine on Saints QB Kenny Stabler for a safety. Cromwell then intercepted a pass and rambled 43 yards for a touchdown in the fourth quarter. Finally, the entire Ram defense held on fourth down late in the game, setting up Mike Lansford's winning field goal with just two seconds left. On to Dallas!

It was Ferragamo who took over in the first playoff game, drilling TD strikes to David Hill, Preston Dennard and George Farmer. The Rams clouted the Cowboys, 24-17.

Now, the dream was becoming clearer and clearer, closer and closer. Could the surprising Rams repeat their fairy-tale finish of 1979? The dream turned to a nightmare when the Washington Redskins unleashed their hogs. The Rams were gobbled up, 51-7, and their season was over.

Coach Robinson's Rams came back with fire in their eyes in 1984, with Dickerson blazing the trail. Dickerson, who wears big, thick eyeglasses with jet-black frames, looks more like a college professor than a football star. In 1984, however, he showed once again that looks are deceiving.

Game by game, Dickerson carved up the Rams' book of records, and he did it in the most outrageous way possible. Opposing defenses knew that Dickerson would be running at their ends. They knew he would attempt to turn the corner and tightrope down the sideline. They knew he was coming, and they were right there in bunches to stop him, but Dickerson would still breeze right on past them.

Did you know?

Tight-end Mike Barber, who came to the Rams from the Oilers in 1982, is an active member of the Fellowship of Christian Athletes and devotes a weekend each month to helping prison inmates change their lives.

> **Did you know?**
>
> *Coach John Robinson took the Rams to a respectable 9-7 season in his first year (1983), and followed it up with a 10-6 record and a trip to the playoffs in '84. Robinson was named Coach of the Year in the NFC in '83 and hailed by experts throughout the country for his successcul transition from college coaching to the NFL.*

In the 15th game of the season, the entire nation looked on in wonder as Dickerson actually eclipsed one of the most revered records in the NFL—O.J. Simpson's 2,003-yard rushing mark! Dickerson's new record of 2,105 yards may stand for years to come...that is, if Dickerson doesn't break it himself.

It was fortunate for the Rams that Dickerson was running so well. Ferragamo was injured and lost early in the season. The starting QB role fell to Jeff Kemp, who had been a fourth-string QB three years earlier. The experts predicted failure for Kemp, but Jeff surprised everyone but himself by leading the Rams to a 10-6 record and a second-straight post-season berth.

"When Ferragamo went down, even I had my doubts about the playoffs," admitted Robinson. "But these guys keep surprising me. They are really fun to be around. They work really hard, and they come back every week."

DON'T GO AWAY!

Heading into the second half of the 1980's, the Rams' fans had every reason to renew their season tickets. For starters, the new cross-town rivalry between the Rams and the Raiders was beginning to resemble the pistol-packing feud between the Hatfields and the McKoys.

"The Raiders like to howl at the moon," shrugged Vince Ferragamo, "but all the noise in the world won't make the moon go away. They can growl and howl all they want, but the Rams will still be right here waiting for them."

Jeff Kemp emerged from the shadow of Vince Farragamo in 1985.

Ferragamo's confidence was echoed by a powerful nucleus of Rams veterans, including Jack Youngblood, Nolan Cromwell, Drew Hill and others. Streaking close behind them were the youngsters—rising stars like Leroy Irvin, Gary Green, Reggie Doss and, of course, Eric Dickerson. Speedster Ron Brown was there, and so was former Canadian All-Star quarterback, Dieter Brock.

The stage was set, the stars were in their places. Once again, it was showtime in L.A.

Did you know?

Georgia Frontiere, the dynamic president and owner of the Rams, is one of the few women who hold top management positions in the NFL. She is admired throughout the league for the bold way in which she has streamlined the daily operations of the Rams' organization—and for her continued devotion to several charities.

Fleet-footed Eric Dickerson leaves another one grasping at thin air in '84.

Silver Creek School
Library